# COME TO THE FEAST

# COME TO THE FEAST
## An Invitation to Eucharistic Transformation

*Richard N. Fragomeni, Ph.D.*

CONTINUUM • NEW YORK

2000

The Continuum Publishing Company
370 Lexington Avenue
New York, NY 10017

Printed in the United States of America

**Library of Congress Cataloging-in-Publication Data**

Fragomeni, Richard N.
    Come to the feast : an invitation to eucharistic
transformation / Richard Fragomeni
        p.    cm.
    ISBN  0-8264-1129-0
    1. Lord's Supper—Catholic Church.    I. Title.
BX2215.2F73    1998
264'.02036—dc21                                    97-15778
                                                            CIP

John Shea's poem "The prayer of the Holy Sacrifice of
the Mass" from the book *The Hour of the Unexpected* is
reprinted with the permission of the publisher.
Copyright © 1992 by John Shea. Published by Thomas
More, A Division of RCL, Resources for Christian
Living, 200 East Bethany Drive, Allen, TX 75002

*For my mother and father*

# CONTENTS

# 1

# The Overwhelming Gift

*A new heart I will give you, and a new spirit I will put within you; and I will remove from your body the heart of stone and give you a heart of flesh. I will put my spirit within you, and make you follow my statutes and be careful to observe my ordinances.*

*—Ezechiel 36:26–27*

Once I went to Mass with my aunt. The liturgy was lifeless and boring. *Lousy* was the term my aunt used, as I recall. Singing was largely absent, the homily grew worse by the minute, and it went on for many minutes. I sat fidgeting in the pew, growing angrier with each liturgical outrage, and finally, at the end of Mass, I asked my aunt, "You put up with this every week?" She replied serenely, "Sweetie, the problem with you is you pay attention."

Then she made me promise that if I ever had the opportunity to work with the liturgy of the church, I would help people to understand it in such a way that folks like her wouldn't have to turn off their hearing aids. May she rest in peace.

I offer this little volume as a partial fulfillment of that promise. I'll keep the rest of the promise with my time teaching liturgy—for now, at least, in Chicago at Catholic Theological Union.

I address this book to your heart as much as to your head. Plain information is helpful, but often it doesn't change hearts. Liturgy can change our hearts. I believe that the starting place for the transformation of our lives and the way we think begins in our hearts. I'm writing this to help with the process of creating a fully human heart promised by Ezechiel and fulfilled in authentic liturgy.

When I talk about hearts, I mean the center of our personalities. Recall the story from Detroit a few years ago. A father received a heart transplant from his daughter. He was waiting for a transplant when his daughter was killed in a car accident. He received the tragic news of her death with the information that her heart would be his if he wanted it. He received his own daughter's heart, and from that moment on, her heart would keep him alive. He is reported to have said recently that he believes his daughter is not dead; she lives within him.

In a real way, God takes our stony hearts and puts in us the heart of Jesus, so that our lives can be changed. As our hearts are changed, we hope our thinking will change. If our hearts and our heads change, perhaps we can make some new decisions about what it means to be fully human, fully alive in a human way. That was St. Irenaeus's definition of a Christian—someone fully alive. He said that was the real glory of God.

If our hearts are changed by God, if we're open to that power, then our behaviors change. If that happens, little by little our families, our communities, and the world change. The heart of the world can change, starting with us. We can stop being such bitter, hardhearted people, and we can thaw these cold and bitter times.

## The Mystery

My starting point is the gift of God. What is it like to receive a gift? Jack Shea, a Chicago theologian and storyteller, has written a little poem about the Mass. It reaches my heart; I hope it will touch yours. His title is very official-sounding.

The Prayer of the Holy Sacrifice of the Mass

Those who do not believe in a Higher Harmony
will balk when told an accident crunched
in the parking lot at the very moment
the altar boy's nose began to bleed.
He bled on the surplice, the cassock,

the candle, the other altar boy,
and the priest's unlaced shoe
which bulgingly carried an Ace bandaged ankle.
The priest was stuffing a purificator up the
    boy's nose,
damning the blood into his eyeballs,
when the lector asked, "how do you pronounce
E-l-i-s-h-a" and the organist pounded
the entrance "Praise to the Lord."

They processed.
The bleeding, the halt, and the mute
unto the altar of God.

Saturday was late and liquored
and delivered God's people,
sunglassed and slumping, to the epilogue
of weekend life, the Gothic Church.
They were not the community of liberal theology
nor the scrubbed inhabitants of filmstrips.
They were one endless face
and that face was asleep.

"May the grace of our Lord . . ."

A hungry pause for repentance.
A quick feast of sins.

The lector murdered the prophets once again
and bypassed the section where a certain
    E-l-i-s-h-a
was having prophetic truck with a widow.
The homily parlayed a fairly clear gospel
(you are either with me or against me)
into sentences of vacillation

and paragraphs of double-think.
The priest ran to the Creed for refuge
only to find a special creed was prepared
for this morning's liturgy by Mrs. Zardek
"I believe in butterflies and the breath of . . ."

. . . . . . . . . . . . . . . . . . . . . . . . . . . . . . . . . . . . . . . . . . . . . . . . . . . . . . . . . .

The offertory gifts never made it.
They were dropped by an elderly couple
("We never liked the new Mass anyway.")
who collided with a small but speedy child
whose highheeled mother was in klicky-klack
      pursuit
and whose name was "Rodgercomeback."

The consecration was consistent.
The priest lifted the host
and said, "This is my blood."
Instantly aware of his eucharistic goof
but also momentarily in the grip of a bizarre
      logic
he changed the wine into Jesus' body.
Then
with his whole mind, heart, and soul
he genuflected
      — never to rise —
to a mystery which masks itself
as mistake
and a power which perfects itself
in weakness.

So when I write of God's invitation to
accept the gift, the mystery we never quite rise

to, I know these thoughts are feeble and humble attempts at reaching beyond understanding to a mystery. A finger pointing to the moon.

It is a mystery for us who are baptized. A mystery that is not incomprehensible, but it is a mystery that is infinitely comprehensible. A mystery is not a puddle of muddy water into which we can't see. No, it is more like an absolutely pure mountain lake that is so deep that no matter how much we see its purity, we cannot see to the bottom. That means the more we understand with our hearts, the more we understand how much more there is to understand about what we think we now know.

We approach the mystery that can never be exhausted by conversation, or catechism, by doctrine, or any experience. We live in the mystery that we can't comprehend as a fish lives in the ocean it cannot fathom.

So we approach as the priest in the story, genuflecting, never quite rising fully. We don't ever respond adequately to the invitation to the feast, to the presence of God, who wants to give us all new hearts.

Don't be like the woman who came to confession. She said, "Bless me, Father, I have not sinned." "Oh?" I said. "No, I have not sinned. I've made it." "Made it to what?" I asked. "I've made it to sanctity. I'm a saint." So I asked, "Why are you coming to confession?" She said, "Simply to inform you of the matter."

I don't think so. I think we never quite make it. But the attempt is exhilarating and makes us human.

The gift is given in the mystery—the unsayable, said; the unfathomable, fathomed.

## The Experience of Gift

We must start with analogy when we talk about the mystery of God. Our analogies are human, because that is the way all incarnational theology begins. We believe in the incarnation of God as Jesus. So within our human experience we can find traces of this mystery.

Begin with the experience of receiving a gift. Have you ever received an overwhelming one? I'm talking about the kind that leaves you breathless; the kind that, when you open it, you ask, "Why did you do that?" About the kind that leaves you saying, "You shouldn't have done this, I don't have one for you!" I'm talking about the kind that reduces you to silence . . . or perhaps, tears. Some of you have had a gift like that. I like to give those extravagant gifts sometimes, just to make people feel overwhelmed. There's something awkward about that experience, isn't there? About being overwhelmed. Often at Christmas, I protect myself against that experience. I prepare so that cannot happen, so that I won't be overwhelmed by a gift I can't reciprocate. I buy three or four gifts and put them away. Then, if someone gives me a gift, and I am embarrassed and overwhelmed, I say, "Excuse me." Then I can go into my bedroom, slip on a gift tag, and say without blushing, "This is for you." But it doesn't really work. Not all gifts come wrapped.

I remember a few years ago, when I was working in a parish in Albany and a woman came to me who had a miscarriage in her first pregnancy. That is so painful. I've had to speak to many women who have had this tragedy. It is not only painful, but it is confusing. They feel inadequate, angry with God. Why should, why would this happen? What's life all about? So this woman came to my office, and I let her scream at God. (She had gone to a couple of other ministers who had informed her it was "God's will." Of course, she couldn't handle that.) But she was screaming and I said, "Scream it out. If God can't accept it, who can?" (I do that occasionally myself. The psalms do it all the time. They dignify their screaming by labeling them Lamentation Psalms, but screaming is screaming.) Even Jesus on the cross quotes a lamentation psalm: "Why did you forsake me?" (Psalm 22:1). So I encouraged her to scream. After that, she went home feeling more at peace with God. Later she said to me (and I'll never forget this), "Father, if my husband and I get pregnant again, we want you to be there." After I recovered and asked what she meant, she explained that she and her husband wanted me to be present at the

*The Overwhelming Gift*

birth of their child. "We want you to be there, in the room, when the baby is born. We know you probably won't have a child of your own, and this would be our gift to you." I've been around a long time, but I was speechless—and upon reflection a little dubious. Still I thought it was a wonderful gift, and so I was with them during her 18 hours of labor. And I was there when the baby was born. That was 9 years ago, and I'm still overwhelmed by their doing that for me, because I would never have that experience as a priest.

But the gift that touched me most deeply was one I received just this last Christmas. There is a little old Italian lady, Angelina. She is on a fixed income. Fixed income is the politically correct term for suffering from poverty. She has no family, no husband, and no children. Angelina ducks into the church on Christmas Day and sees me. She says, "I'm glad you're back. I've been saving up all year for you. See me after Mass." So I see her after Mass, give her a kiss, and she pulls out a little card. "It's for you." I tell her "thank you" and put it in my pocket. After Christmas Mass I go home, take off my coat, and discover the card. I open it up and see that she's written, "To my favorite priest, you always treat me like a queen." And there were three one-dollar bills. Three dollars—and she saved all year to give me these! I was overwhelmed. I would have had a heart of stone not to have cried.

I think that's the kind of human experience that must touch our bones if we really want to come to the feast, if we really expect to be born again, like Nicodemus in John's Gospel. If we're going to be reborn, renewed, and tranformed, we must let the experience of being overwhelmed by love in our human lives get through to us.

Sometimes we block it. We block the overwhelming gift, because in twentieth-century America it does something unaccustomed to our psyche.

Especially to men. Men are trained by our culture to be in control, to be their own persons, to be in charge. We are taught subtly that to maintain a modicum of order in our lives, we must call the shots. To receive the overwhelming gift to which we have no reciprocal response, to be powerless in the exchange, makes us vulnerable. That's why I buy the extra gifts at Christmas. I dislike being vulnerable. To be unable to match gift for gift puts us in the down position. Most unmanly.

The liturgy invites us into a sense of unconditional love. But these days in our United States culture, we are suspicious of the unconditional. We've been taught good capitalism—there is no free lunch. So if someone overwhelms me with a gift, my first reaction is cultural—"What do they want?" Or, just as cynically, "What did they do?" And if they're Catholic, "Did they take pleasure in it?"

*The Overwhelming Gift*

It can be difficult to receive an overwhelming gift, because it invites us into a sense of deep wonder at who we are to be so graced with this gift. I stood there Christmas night in tears, asking, "Who am I that this woman saves all year to give me such wealth. Who am I that they allow me to be there to hear the baby's first cries? It makes we wonder if they really knew who I am? Would I be so gifted if they knew? Or is the gift that unconditional?" Thus, finally, I think the overwhelming gift brings me to a sense of true humility. Mark this in your etymological dictionary or in your "word save." The word *humility* comes from the Latin *humus,* which means *dirt* or *earth*. To be truly humble is to realize that we are earth. Ashes. Mortal. But, in humility, we also find our true humanity, because *humanity* comes from the same word. And in our humanity/humility, we can find the other *humus* cognate, *humor*. Laughter and joy. To receive the overwhelming gift in humility, in vulnerability, in unconditional love, in deep wonder—all these unleash true joy within us. If, of course, we can allow ourselves to be vulnerable.

This is a tough order, a demanding psychic shift. We live in a world that doesn't teach us how to be vulnerable, human, or humble, or even open to wonder and awe. But that's what is required for liturgy. That is the human analogue that allows us to enter into what the mystics experience when they stand before God.

They say, *nada*, "nothingness." It's the experience of the great saints of our tradition who did the same. They said and felt, "We are nothing, God. You are God. We are not." It's the experience that grounds the receptivity we must have when we come to the feast.

It is a stretch, difficult and subtle, to make Christianity a way of life rather than just a set of religious practices. Christian life demands that we be receptive and vulnerable and open to being flooded with a gift, to be humble and human. Who really wants that? Isn't that part of what the Genesis temptation is all about? In the poetic account of the first temptation, we see that our ancestors received the overwhelming gift of living in a garden. The garden was too much for them. It was too risky and too vulnerable and too humiliating to be overwhelmed by such gifts. They had to eat of the tree of the knowledge of good and evil, so they could know what they could do and could not do, so they could earn their garden by being good. They had to take matters into their own hands. They made the momentous decision to play God, to be in control. Merely standing in receptivity to the gift was more than they could handle.

In the presence of any gift, we face the urge to *take* it, not have it *given* to us. We can do this by taking it for granted; *quid pro quo*, which we can freely translate as tit for tat. It feels so, well, settled. Gifts are unsettling.

In a world that says on good days we are entitled to what we earn and on bad days entitled to what we can take, we are pilgrims. In our more than real world, the symbolic world of the liturgy, we enter a world of gift in which we receive everything without reference to entitlement. We are helpless to take; if we try to take, we offend. When we try to take the gift, we destroy its nature. We only can receive this as gift.

I do believe we can learn to receive and to allow ourselves to be overwhelmed by God as gift. It is a learning of the heart, it isn't taught in schools, but it can be absorbed in the quietude of prayer.

The real reason we repeat the liturgy each week is to learn to receive. Furthermore, that's why we observe Lent each year. We do it every year, trying to get it right. We learn over and over that we are people of dust to whom everything has been given. On some level, we know this is true so we crowd churches on Ash Wednesday. We stand in line to be told to "Remember, you are dust and to dust you will return." We know that's the truth the world will not tell us, we know this is the only place we'll hear this truth. As soon as we go outside church, we run into ads that promise us perpetual youth if we buy what they're selling. And they're lying.

The symbol reaches us and tells us the truth that gives us life, gives us the courage to accept our deaths. We know down deep that if we embrace our *humus-ness*, we will be vulnerable and awestruck and open to receive the gift of God. Then we experience, at least for a moment, that it is no longer we that live, but Christ who lives within us.

## Who Is This God?

Who is this God we learn to know through the experience of extraordinary gift? Our God is an extraordinary god. There is no god like our God. People often say, to win arguments or placate powers, "Well, we all believe in the same God." I don't think so. There may be a superficial agreement on the word, but our image of God is not the same as most. Begin with our belief in the Trinity. Our God is not like the monotheistic deity of Judaism or Islam. Allah is the one God and Yahweh is the one God, but our God is Triune, and that has enormous consequences as we try to find out what our God is like.

Ancient Roman iconography used triangles; Greek iconography used concentric circles. However, the best understanding of what the Trinity might be like, our best analogy, is that of the dance. The Greek word to describe how the three persons in the Trinity interrelate is *perichoresis*. (From which we get our word choreograph; you know what a choreographer is—someone who designs dances.) Our God is a dance of love, a mutual exchanging of personalities, a mutual exchange of gifts. The Father gives to the Son, and the Son gives to the Father, and that experience is so real that it is a person, the Holy Spirit. The Trinity is the dance of the ebb and flow of a God whose very nature is to give God's self. God is love, but one can't do that without another and so the nature of our Trinity—God is the God who pours out gifts—overwhelmingly. Our understanding of God is so dynamic that we see God as constantly giving to all creation. God so loved the world that the Son was given, and the Son so loved us that he poured himself out on the mystery of the cross. When he did, he poured out the Spirit on us. This Spirit so abides in us that when we are together, we become the very place of God's outpouring gift to the world. That's our unbelievable belief.

But I didn't grow up with the image of this dancing, giving, outpouring God. Did you? I grew up in a Jansenistic, Italian-American community. (Jansenism, as it was felt in this country, was a heresy that viewed God as ultra-demanding, cold, and punitive. It was a heresy that substituted fear for love. The first consequence was a rigorous moral code that was impossible to fulfill.) Everything was a sin, God was out to get me. He was making a list and checking it twice, gonna find out who's naughty and nice. I went to confession constantly, *because* practically everything I did was a sin.

Before I made my confirmation, I went to confession six times.

Because I was so bad, God didn't love me; I had to make God love me. I had to perform my best to do things that would earn God's stingy love. My mother took full advantage of my bad theology. "If God did all these things for you, the least you can do is go to church for fifty minutes." This reciprocity assumes that we who are dust can make some kind of bargain with the creator of the universe. We tried. I tried.

This is not the God of our tradition, the God who is the overflowing gift to those who are able to acknowledge that the only life they have is what God has given freely. Instead, we have the old man, the young man, and the bird. Or he/she/it is a supreme being who is a spirit without gender, and if you look closely, not much else, either (*Baltimore Catechism*, Revised Edition, Number 3). So it is with some torque of our soul that we come to the liturgy to meet the God whose nature is to overflow in an overwhelming gift, the extraordinary gift to which our only response can be receptive gratitude.

It feels too good to be true. God is overflowing with the gift of God's self for me. That's hard to believe. When I think of Angelina, I say to myself, "Well, if Angelina really knew me, maybe she wouldn't give me that gift." But when I bring that attitude into the experience of God, it gets tough, because God really knows us. Knows our secrets, has easy access to every skeleton in our closets. Knows when we've been even less than human in our behaviors, hearts, and choices.

Yet, this is our faith. This God of infinite mystery is a God who keeps flooding us precisely because we are sinners. Precisely because we are broken, unfinished ashes and dust, with dirty hands and hearts. This God overflowed so Nicodemus could be born again, not returned to his mother's womb. Nicodemus couldn't grasp the mystery. He was dense, wanting to maintain control. "What do you mean, born again?" Basically he said, "I don't believe in overwhelming gift." Jesus insisted. "No, Nicodemus, this really is overwhelming gift, this is the Holy Spirit and it is from God, the God who so loved the world." All Nicodemus would have to do is open his hands and receive it. But that was too much for him. And for us? Those who know how to do that are usually those who have hit rock bottom and discovered they are but dust and ashes. (That's why I love to deal with people in 12-step programs. To get into a 12-step program, you must know you are at rock bottom. Then you surrender everything to the one who floods and who knows you, and nevertheless offers you the gift for you to receive.)

That's a wonderful way of knowing God. I love that God. I could not love, could not warm up to, the one I always had to confess to and who had the list and who probably had fire coming out the mouth.

That image of God couldn't hold people. So from the sixteenth century forward, our tradition developed a long, strong relationship with Mary. In effect, she became our source of gift. We prayed to her, we loved her, we had all sorts of devotions to her, because we felt within that she was the image of unconditional love. She carried this truth on an emotional level. In the cold world run by a supreme being, we needed the warmth of a mother's love, we needed the experience of unconditional love.

Mary is still important in the world of the Trinity, but she doesn't have to remind us of what is missing, she can point to the depth of what is offered. She is not the source of love, but she is an enormously rich example of how to say, "let it be done to us" . . . a way of receiving the gift.

## Christ Is God's Gift to Us

Christ is God's incarnate invitation to the feast. Christ is God's outpouring love among us. Christ is God's gift of bread to us. Christ is God's gift of mercy poured out to sinners. If you keep your heart focused on Christ, you see the gift given even to Zacchaeus, the short taxpayer up a tree, the gift given to Mary Magdalene who had to deal with seven devils. Christ was a gift given to Lazarus who was stinking in the tomb and to the lepers no one else would touch. He was gift to the sinners and tax collectors, and the woman caught in adultery.

He was gift to the slumpy, sleepy apostles, to Peter who was called *Rock* and was discovered to be mush a lot of the time. Christ is the gift of God's outpouring love on everyone, even enemies. This is the singular quality of God's gift of Christ—it extends even to enemies and to us when we make ourselves enemies by our sin.

There is one sinister move that we can make to turn Christ into our judge rather than our gift. We can become self-righteous. If we manage self-righteousness, then we say and act like we don't need any gifts—or want any, for that matter. So when we refuse the gifts, they are refused. That's a problem with gifts, they can't be taken and they can't be forced. The self-righteous do both.

The self-righteous don't just refuse the gifts for themselves. That would be bad enough; they also try to deny the gift to others. "He doesn't deserve the gift. He's divorced. She shouldn't be allowed to the gift table, she's had an abortion. And this one is black and that one gay. Communities need standards, you know. If everyone belongs, then the gift is cheapened and it doesn't mean anything to be Catholic any-more." You've heard your own variations on this dreary theme.

Once we're in charge of who gets the gifts, we also feel in charge of who not only should not be given gifts but condemned to live without what they have. I learned to swear and con-demn folks when I moved to Chicago and met them in traffic. I had a pure mouth when I came, but I learned to swear like a trooper when I hit the traffic on the Kennedy Freeway. "Go to hell," I would scream at someone who cut me off. "Go to hell." When we say that, what do we mean? We mean they don't deserve the gift of God. In Latin it is "*Anathema sit*," and we have said it to many.

We forget that Christ received everyone, except those who by themselves declined to receive the gift. Christ offers the gift to all, the gift from God is given to all—overwhelmingly. We can refuse it and self-righteousness be-comes the central way of refusal.

I find it hard to believe that we would refuse the gift. That's why I always thought it was hard to commit a moral sin when I was a kid, even though I believed I committed them every day. How hard it is to be cut off from life.

So I've made a resolution that now when I'm on the freeway I won't decide who should receive the gift and who shouldn't. I can't de-cide that because God is God, and I am not. So now when they pass me, cut me off, just drive outrageously, or when I am in a jam and they're all around me, I say, "Bless you." Because that's the gift—to be a blessing, not a curse. And Jesus says, "Bless your enemies." Bless those who would cut you off. Bless those who persecute you (even on the freeway). Bless those who differ from you. Let them be a blessing to you. In this, they will know that you are the children of God, and you are my disciples. If you love one another and wash one another's feet, you become your true self. We become the very place where Christ continues to flow into the world and into history. We, in turn, become God's gift by having so deeply received it.

So God's invitation has taken flesh in Jesus, and we must see how he invited people to come to the feast—lavishly.

## The Gift Is a Surprise

A gift is inherently a surprise. It is no accident that we wrap gifts. Wrapping is to hide the gift until the precise moment when it can surprise. We are wired for surprise. It makes our blood rise, our hearts beat faster. Being surprised by God is a homely definition of hope.

I think that is the real message of the parable of the Good Samaritan (Luke 10:29–37). We often moralize from that parable, telling folks that we, too, should take care of strangers in the ditch. But the story is about the man in the ditch. He would have expected help from the priest and Levite, but when the Samaritan would take care of him, he would have had an experience that would teach him that the gift of God can come from the most surprising quarters. He never knew God could deliver salvation in such an unlikely package. Neither do we.

We want to be open to the surprise of the unexpected gift, the overwhelming gift. Some of us have this surprise mechanism thwarted in our childhood by disappointment. Have you had this happen to you? You're in a crowd and someone looks at you and waves. You're surprised, but you wave back. Then the person looks at you more closely, and you see disappointment on the faces. You were not the expected person—the one wanted! If we get disappointed a lot in our surprises, sooner or later we learn not to like them, because we've been hurt too often. We get pumped up with anticipation and then our balloon gets punctured, and we are left flat. And we go through life flat.

But surprise is our emotional starting point. Our inner eyes are suddenly opened in amazement when we realize that everything is gift. The world, our lives, our loves, even to the point where we see that we are ourselves gifts of God. When this sinks in, and we can be mindful of it, our hearts absorb it. Then our

*The Overwhelming Gift*

world comes alive and everything becomes gift. In that mindfulness, we are grateful Eucharistic people.

In gratefulness, we are fully alive to a gratuitously given world. We understand ourselves, then, to be the channel through which the gift of God continues to be given to the world. We become church, channel, and sacrament of gratitude as God continues to pour out an extravagant promise to the world.

# 2

# Surrender to the Gift

*Beginning with Moses and all the prophets, he interpreted to them the things about himself in all the scriptures.*

*—Luke 24:27*

Come with me down the road to Emmaus (Luke 24:13–35). Read the story carefully several times, and I'll comment on it. The two disciples are Cleopas and someone whose name we don't know. It was probably his wife. Remember his wife, Mary, was at the foot of the cross with Jesus. So Cleopas and his wife are walking out of Jerusalem feeling pretty bad about things and Jesus appears to them. Among other things, he opens up the scriptures. It must have been a long conversation, because it says he opened up Moses and all the prophets. Do you know how many prophets there are?

Then Jesus seems to be leaving, but they say, "Oh, no, it's late. Come and stay with us." They were receptive and vulnerable to the gift of this stranger. So Jesus sat at table, took bread and broke it, and they recognized him. But he vanished from their eyes. They rise, filled with this gift, and go out and preach that the Lord has risen. They tell the other disciples that they have recognized him in the breaking of the bread.

The Emmaus story is an interpretation of the ritual and the discipline of the Eucharistic assembly. It is what modern theologians call a mystagogical reading of the Sunday celebration. I love the word *mystagogical*. It means it is a story that interprets what we do on Sunday. If you put the structure of the Mass right next to the story, you see they are parallel. The Emmaus story interprets us more then we interpret the story. What happens to the disciples is what can happen to us. We do what they did so that God will do for us what he did for them—interpret the scriptures and leave our hearts burning and witnessing to the presence of the Risen Lord.

### Real Presence

The first thing that happens on the road to Emmaus is Jesus' appearance. They are bewildered, and he offers them an interpretation of life by offering them the scriptures. So it is with us. Week after week, we come to the liturgy, and we sit and listen to the scriptures. We

*Surrender to the Gift*

believe that the real presence of the Risen Lord is being communicated to us through these. Vatican II in the Constitution on the Sacred Liturgy (Paragraph 7) expanded our notion of the *real presence*. Until then, Catholics believed in the real presence, but confined it to the tabernacle. We still believe it is in the tabernacle, because we believe in the real presence of Christ in the Eucharist. But the council expanded real presence to include whenever the Word is proclaimed. Jesus walks with us on the road to Emmaus. There is real presence in the community of people as we hear together what Christ is proclaiming to us.

The council also teaches that Christ is present in the ministers of the church and, of course, in the celebration of all the sacraments—"where two or three are gathered in my name" (Matt. 18:20). The real presence of Christ in the Eucharist has been expanded to include the various types of real presence in Word, sacrament, and community.

The first thing we do on Sunday is hear this Word. What Word? The same story, over and over, of the gift of God to us. It's the story of our God whose nature is gift from beginning to end. The liturgy of the Word is like grand opera. It's the same story every time. In the opera, this one falls in love, it's unrequited, she shoots him, and kills herself in a suitably dramatic way. Same story every time. Why do we keep going? To feel the depth of the story.

As we come to the liturgy week after week, Jesus continues to tell us the same story about the gift. Remember those difficult readings in the fifth chapter of Matthew after the Beatitudes that say, "If you get angry with your brother and sister in your heart, you are a liar and a murderer. If you even think lustful thoughts [remember Jimmy Carter?] you've committed adultery in your heart. If you have any gift to give your neighbor, leave it behind and go be reconciled, then come back. Then your holiness will go beyond the scribes and Pharisees" (Matt. 5:21–25).

Why did Jesus tell us that? Because he's not only talking about what we should be doing, he's talking about what God has already done. Our God has already gone beyond. Beyond the holiness prescribed by the regulations of the scribes and the Pharisees. What is being proclaimed is a moral code based on the example of our God's way of treating us. You might say our God goes beyond even what is expected of God, so we are called to more than would usually be expected of us.

So, week after week, the readings that gather us at the Sunday celebration are there to offer us a vision of God's world. The readings throw out balls—*symballs*. Actually, the word *symbol* comes from the Greek word meaning "to throw together." Some balls we catch, others we miss for a while, at least. But when you catch one in your heart, you're "it." You're changed forever. Another way to say it is that the Word of God is like a "two-edged sword" (Hebrews 4:12) that also pierces our heart and changes it. We catch the Word, the symbols, in our imagination. What is presented in the readings and preaching is nothing less than the world as it is in God's imagination. We are given an image of the hidden plan of God. We are encouraged to form our imaginations according to God's imagination. God's imagination is the way it can be if we are grateful for the gift, the way the world can be if we allow God to surprise us with a new way to be human, the real way to be human. Week after week, we are shown facets of this imaginative picture of God's world.

In one sense it's like an advertisement, a pitch. Week after week, the liturgy advertises on the billboard, "here's how God's world looks." "Here's what our God is like." It takes weekly repetition for that to sink in. The problem, of course, is that day after day and hour after hour we are bombarded by other advertisements that say the world is otherwise. And these ads have their moral codes, instructions for conduct to conform to that world view. Our imaginations are polluted with symbols that instruct us in grasping, not giving. We hear through every medium things like "Let K-Mart be your savings place." If you think Jesus saves, you should see K-Mart! A Buick becomes something to believe in. This will save you, that will give you infinite sex appeal, and these will make you happy beyond your fondest dreams. Brush with, comb with, polish with, wear, drive, and drink this, and everyone will want to kiss you!

But once a week, Jesus walks with us on the road to Emmaus and interprets our lives in view of another, a new vision. And blessed are they who have ears to hear what they hear. We Catholics aren't good at this yet. We were trained that the only thing we had to do on Sunday to "fulfill our obligation" was to be present for the offertory, consecration, and communion. We weren't trained to have the scriptures, the proclaimed Word, interpret our lives. That's still a stretch. Many parishes are offering lectionary and bible study opportunities to help the community prepare for the Sunday assembly. This is a positive step toward hearing God's Word together.

Now the renewed liturgy asks us to reconsider radically the role of hearing the Word that Jesus spoke to the disciples at Emmaus. It asks us to acknowledge that the Word is lifegiving. The prophet Isaiah says that what comes from God's mouth does not return empty.

> For as the rain and snow come down from heaven, and do not return there until they have watered the earth, making it bring forth and sprout, giving seed to the sower and bread to the eater, so shall my word be that goes out

from my mouth; it shall not return to me empty, but it shall accomplish that which I purpose, and succeed in the thing for which I sent it. (Isaiah 55:10–11)

But, as with all powerful things, we should be careful. Annie Dillard observes that "If you knew what God's Word can do to you, you'd wear a crash helmet in church." If we allow that powerful word to reach us, then our hearts, like those of the disciples on the road to Emmaus, will burn within us with the promise and the hope of what could be if God is God.

## The Eucharistic Prayer

After the Word presents us with a vision of the way the world could be, a world in which the poor will be blessed, the meek will be blessed, and even those who are persecuted for justice' sake will be blessed, we move to the next part of the liturgy. We bring the bread and wine to the table and pray the great Eucharistic prayer. After the proclamation of the Word of God to us, we respond by gathering around the table and praising God.

Jesus sat at table with the apostles, took bread and broke it; blessed God, thanked God, and praised God. That's the second movement of the liturgy. We do this week after week. We bring bread and wine to the table. It's not only bread and wine on the table, it's the community around the table that is brought to prayer. The prayer begins, "The Lord be with you." "Lift up your hearts." "Let us give thanks to the Lord our God." "Father, we thank you and praise you. We thank you for this opportunity to gather. We thank you for the Word you have proclaimed to us and vision you give us every week. We praise you through Jesus who has offered to us your gift of life. We praise you for the Spirit and so with the angels we sing your praise." A whole tapestry of praise. "From the beginning you loved us, we praise you. Because you have sent your Spirit, we praise you. You now continue to send your Spirit, the Spirit that brings us your gift, so we praise you. We praise you in Jesus Christ who, on the night before he died, took bread and said, 'This is my body. This is my blood.' We praise you for Christ, we remember his death and resurrection. We anticipate the day he will come again in glory and we praise you with all the church. We praise you with the saints, with all the dead. On that day of fulfillment, we shall see you as you are, we will be like you and sing your praises forever. We thank you." You get the point. This is a prayer of praise and thanksgiving—a Eucharistic prayer.

At the end, we pray this through Christ and in Christ, in the power of the Holy Spirit, all glory and honor be yours, Almighty God, forever and ever. And the people "Amen." In this Amen, we give ourselves to God. It is the final acclamation of our praise.

## Praise and Thanksgiving

When we offer this prayer, what are we doing? When we praise something, what is going on inside us? I love Dolly Parton, the country and western singer. "Dolly, I love you; I praise you, Dolly; I thank you, Dolly; thank you for your music, you are absolutely wonderful." I've become a fan. The word *fan* is short for *fanatic*. I go to the Cubs's games. I praise them on occasion. What am I doing?

Something happens inside us when we give praise. When we praise, we surrender to the beauty of the other. Praise and thanks are acts of surrender to the beauty of the gift you are receiving. Praise is surrender. Thanks opens us to receive the gift.

In the early church, to become a bishop, you had to have two talents. The first was to be able to preach up a storm and the second was to be able to pray up a storm. They had no books to read Eucharistic prayers from. So bishops would gather around the table and start praising and praying. Guess what they used for source material? Readings from the first part of the liturgy. They took those stories, names, images, and themes and turned them into prayer. You get a glimpse of that early practice in our prefaces, especially those for Lent. We pray about the Samaritan woman at the Eucharistic table that we read about a few minutes before. The bishops were made bishops, because they could connect vision and prayer. Really, in a sense, when we're praising and surrendering to God, we're really praying and surrendering to the vision we just saw in the readings, and receiving the gift of that vision in our lives.

Our hearts burn within us. We come to the table and pray:

> We praise you for this vision you offer us, and we surrender ourselves to you in this vision through Christ. And in the power of the Spirit, we surrender everything to you and to your way of living. We surrender this bread and this wine to you. We surrender our lives to you in praise and thanksgiving and gratitude. It is no longer we who live, but you who live in us.

So when we come to this table, it is an act of surrender that we make to the gift, as we make our prayer of praise. Praise is the surrendering to beauty so the gift can ravish us. In giving thanks, we give nothing to God except our willingness to be overwhelmed by the gift of the feast that we are offered in the Spirit.

## Eating and Drinking

After receiving the vision and surrendering to it in praise, we break the bread and recognize Christ in that act. The bread and the wine have been transformed into the real presence of Christ by the power of the Spirit. "Let your spirit come upon these gifts to make them the body and blood of Christ." We do this every week. Of course, people don't always understand what they are doing, or their attention wanders, and it becomes monotonous, and we repeat "Body of Christ" on automatic pilot. If we were surprised at the gift and could allow our surrender to be real and complete, then the vision would capture our imaginations, and it would not become routine.

The last movement is about eating and drinking. Why do we eat and drink at any time? We do it to celebrate, to share, to do lots of things, but the bottom line is that we eat and drink to survive. If we don't eat and drink, we die. It's sheer survival before it is anything else. Survival is the fundamental drive of our biology.

Survival has an interesting twist to it. We didn't give ourselves life. It was given to us. But rather than receiving life moment by moment, which is scary, we try to take control of our survival. We transform life from a gift to a possession. Then it turns ugly. When we take control of survival, it turns into survival of the fittest. My survival may be at the expense of yours, if I have anything to say about it. Then it becomes my survival against yours.

This twisted notion of survival is not just individual. Groups have it. Think about nationalism: my country over yours. Move to race: whites against blacks, browns against yellows, pick any color, the dynamic is always the same. When survival turns in on itself, we call it Bosnia or the Middle East or any one of many other places. Religious groups are no exceptions. Catholics question Buddhists; Jews and Muslims are at war; and as if that weren't bad enough, we have subdivisions into liberals and conservatives at each other's ideological throats.

It's about survival. Fittingly, bread is another term for money. When we put our trust in money, we move easily into cheating, killing, and stealing for it—things we do to survive. When we come to the table, we come with this twisted notion of survival and this twisted notion of bread that allows us to take life into our own hands.

But when we come to the feast, we eat and drink a new way of surviving. We bring the survival mechanism to God and say, "God, we surrender to you in praise. We surrender to the vision we heard in the reading. We surrender even the survival instinct that would cause us to eat and drink in the old way. We used to eat and drink for ourselves, now we eat and drink

*Surrender to the Gift*

according to the new vision. We accept life as a gift and we accept death as a gift, too."

In a sense, the Eucharist is not the bread of life first. It is first the bread of death. When we come to receive this bread and this cup, we consume the food and drink of death. "When we eat this bread and drink this cup, we proclaim your death." Be careful. It only becomes the bread of life for those who are willing to receive it as the bread of death—death to the ways of surviving that would make us survive on our own terms.

This communion of bread and cup invites us to surrender our survival mechanisms to God, who teaches us that way of surviving with our arms open to receive the gift. We come to realize that we survive not in our own vision but in the vision of a surrender to a word that promises us we will find life if we embrace death.

Can you imagine what the world would be if all of us gave up surviving on our own terms? Can you imagine a world without racism or war? Without racism there would have been no Nazi Germany where the Aryans had to survive over the Jews. What would our cities be like if there were no animosity between blacks and whites? What would our world be like if we were a community where everyone was surviving by giving themselves away? What if we were finding our survival in dying for one another? Where we would be for each other the bread of life? Where we would find our true life by allowing others to eat and drink us? They would recognize the body of Christ, the blood of Christ flowing from the heart of God.

That's why Paul was chiding the Corinthians. "All you Corinthians are coming to dinner here, and you're all feasting on your own. You're stuffing your faces and you're not recognizing the body. And when you do that, you're eating and drinking judgment to yourself."

If we keep on just eating and drinking and using our religion (and sometimes we can use religion) as a way of feeding our own egos, bear in mind what Paul says if we don't stop surviving that way, we'll end up sick.

> For all who eat and drink without discerning the body, eat and drink judgment against themselves. For this reason many of you are weak and ill, and some have died. (1 Cor 11: 29–30)

You know that's true. If all I'm worried about is my self-survival, I get pretty paranoid, weak, and ill. Every week when we come to this table, we are called by it to surrender with open hands even our desire to survive. Symbolically we say, "God, take our basic instinct (because survival is a basic instinct), we surrender it to your vision. Use me as the place where your gift comes."

St. Ignatius of Loyola said it this way:

> Take my memory, my understanding, my imagination, my body, my will, my entire self. God, I give it all to you. Give me only your grace and your love. That is enough.

Imagine getting that right! That's why we come to communion week after week. Until we give up. Then it is no longer we who live, but Christ who lives within us. We have died. So much for survival. In our dying, we find the gift of new life. Our hearts become a symphony of praise.

In fact, we already died in Baptism. We keep on celebrating that death in the Eucharist until we get it right. Like the apostles, we recognize Christ in the breaking of the bread. When we do, then we can go out and proclaim that the Lord is risen. In our deadness, he has made us alive.

This surrender is beyond our power. We can't let go of basic instincts just by an act of will. Liturgy is required, liturgy with all of its symbolic power, is able to coax us into letting go our basic instincts, like the story of George Washington Carver who is said to have been able to convince a cactus to shed its protective needles. He had a mystical relationship with plants, and he communicated to the cactus that it was safe, so it was able to shed it's needles. It's almost as hard for us, but if we have a mystical relationship with God within the liturgy, we can shed our defenses against the gift, too.

It is the Holy Spirit that convinces our hearts and changes our lives.

In traditional theology, when we hear the word *liturgy*, we are told it means the work of the people. It is more than that. It is the work of the people only in the sense that it is something we do to open us up to what God is doing. We may consider liturgy as something we do but that is only about a C+ understanding. We do the ritual, but we hope that in the middle of our doing, God is doing something with us. Our activity expresses our hope that we will be opened up to what God is doing for us and to us, and through us to the world.

I end with a story from Jim Dunning, my mentor and friend.

> Once upon a time, there was a king who was informed by his Lord Chancellor that this year the grain was infected. He said, "If your people eat this grain, they will go crazy. There is not enough grain in the storehouse from last year to feed the whole nation. What shall we do? Have them crazy or starve to death?" Well, that's a tough choice, so the king thought a long time and then responded. "Let the people eat the grain and go crazy. But not all of them. Call some of the people and let them eat the grain from the storehouse so they remain sane. Let those who remain sane be a reminder to those who go crazy that they are crazy. If they remind us crazy ones long enough and hard enough that we are crazy, maybe we will come to our senses again."

Maybe if we understand the vision of the liturgy, it will remind us that we are usually crazy. There is another way to live—in Christ, and Christ takes us to Emmaus each time we come to the feast.

# 3.
# Transformed
# by the Gift

*But you are a chosen race, a royal priesthood, a holy nation, God's own people, in order that you may proclaim the mighty acts of him who called you out of darkness into his marvelous light.*

—*1 Peter 2:9*

$\mathscr{I}$n her poem "Serengeti," named for a beautiful place in Tanzania, the Pulitzer Prize-winning poet Mary Oliver first describes a lion's approach to a water hole, then follows with the lines:

. . . I don't know where I have seen such power before
except perhaps in the chapel where Michelangelo's God,
tawny and muscular, tears the land from the firmament,
and places the sun in the sky so that we may live on
   the earth
among the amazements.
And the lion runs softly through the dusk
and his eyes, under the thick animal lashes, are almost
   tender.

And I don't know when I have been so frightened or so
   happy.

—from *House of Light*
by Mary Oliver
(Beacon Press, 1990)

In the Hebrew scriptures, the Lord God is often
described as the Lion of Judah: powerful, awe-
inspiring, and a being of breath-taking beauty.
In one sense, the element of surprise at the gift
of God can both overwhelm us and bring us
happiness such as we never dreamed can be
given. That gift comes freely from the God who
invites us into a discipline as a church to become a Eucharistic people. We become that
people by hearing, week after week, a word
that envisions a future, a life, a world beyond
what we have created, the world of God's
reign. It is to this world that we surrender our
lives and even our survival mechanism so that
this God can ravish us like the lion of the
Serengeti. When we surrender at the table, we
find ourselves joyful, in a peace the world can
never give. But that's not the whole story.

## Covenant

Our relationship with God is covenantal, not
contractual. In a contract, we spend a great
deal of time, effort, and money on lawyers'

fees, to make sure both sides know what they are getting into. It's there in black and white— read the fine print. When we sign, we sign for a specific obligation and we expect a specific reward.

A covenant is different. We enter into a relationship wherein we have no idea what will be asked of us or what we will receive. It is full of surprises and gifts. So, throughout the history of the church, we've called our marriage vows and our relationship with God not a contract but a covenant. That's why the marriage vow says "for better or worse, richer or poorer." We don't know the terms of agreement, we often say it is like signing a blank check with the amount to be filled in later. We can be present to the gift as gift, because that is our way to integrity of living. In a real sense, that is the way our God is, who chooses to be with us in good times and bad, in sickness and in health, in bread and in stones.

In the midst of whatever life brings, the gift is still given. So even if there is the death of a child, in the midst of our grief, we can know that God is present among us. Out of that, like the phoenix, can come the gift, if we can deal with the stones as well as the bread. The secret is to remain faithful to receiving in gratitude when it gets rough.

Pain and suffering can be gifts. This is subtle and profound. If we are well trained in gratitude when things are good, if we learn how to be open to receive the gift, then we can expand to the point where we can be grateful, even when life is painful. Like Jesus, we can embrace the stones of life, we don't have to turn them into bread. On the other hand, if we've never been grateful for good things, when bad things happen, we will have no capacity for assimilating them.

So when the sun shines, when we get phone calls from our daughters, when our cars are new and our friends are old, when our calendars are not dotted with doctor's appointments, we practice our gratitude for when all those things go into reverse. We do this partially in the hope that we can enter into the mystery of suffering and pain, and find God in the absence of these things. In knowing the presence of God, even in the absence of good things, we then become a gift to those who come to know us in our pain . . . and we in theirs.

It's a sophisticated movement of the soul. That's why I never approach someone in a sickbed, who's been ornery all his or her life and say, "Hey, this is God's gift to you." To those who have learned to cultivate gratitude for life from the beginning, I don't have to say anything. Somehow they have entered into suffering and pain and discovered God there and come out as a prophet. They witness to a new image of God that I can't know, because I'm not in that much pain.

That's a deeper meaning of the Sacrament of the Sick. I don't think the Sacrament of the Sick is just something we do to sick people. We don't anoint the sick, because we want to do something nice for them, even to heal them. I think the sacrament celebrates sickness as a place of revelation of our need and God's gift. We see in the sick and suffering a witness to their ability to see the overwhelming gift of God in the absence of the usual support. They plunge into suffering and come up with new insights into who God is and what life is about, and they emerge more grateful for life. That's the paradox. We anoint them because they are prophets. Anointing the sick is a prophetic anointing. We anoint the sick as if they were Christ on the cross. They are to be a sign for the church that even when they are in the desert with only stones to eat, they are grateful, they know a presence of God in an absence. When you see that, you know it.

We remain as faithful as breath. No matter what happens, we receive the gift of breath. In the scriptures, the Hebrew word *ruah* means breath. The Holy Spirit is given to us as breath is given. Breath is giving and receiving, breathing out and breathing in. We can't hold our breath, we can't clutch the life force. We must surrender to the rhythm and the gift. That is life.

Christ surrendered in that way. In Philippians, we read of the self-emptying of Christ that enables God to give himself to us through Christ.

Let the same mind be in you that was in Christ Jesus, who though he was in the form of God, did not regard equality with God as something to be exploited, but emptied himself, taking the form of a slave, being born in human likeness. (Phil. 2:5–7)

The more we know, the more we know it is mystery that we can't know completely. We know more than we know, and that is humbling. We humbly admit that we are born again and again and again. That's why, throughout our history, we came to the point that we could celebrate Penance again and again. The Sacrament of Penance is a second Baptism—a chance to surrender again to the gift of life.

Members of the early church could confess only once. If they used up their one chance for repentance, they could never confess again, and who knows what might happen to them? But by the twelfth century, we realized, through the Irish monks, that this one forgiveness really wasn't enough. So confession became repeatable and grew into the practice we have today.

### Transformation

We must admit humbly that we don't always capture the mystery completely in that first Baptism. The effects of original sin are still around. Even though original sin is washed away, the effects on our egos remain, and we want to remain strong on our own terms. We want a contract with God, not a covenant. The mystery that allows us indefinitely expanding awareness makes us acknowledge that we are not God, we do not understand or respond completely to the mystery. The covenant God forgives, and we are reborn repeatedly.

We call these rebirths *transformations*, so let's talk about transformation and how it takes place at God's table. We are transformed by the gift at the feast. We are transformed by Christ. What is this transformation? We experience many transformations, but the first is usually the inner movement from blindness to sight. Faith in the scriptures is frequently imaged as the ability to see. Then and now blindness is rampant. Let's look at the story in John's Gospel (Ch. 9) about the man born blind. How many people can't see? Everybody but Jesus and the blind man were unable to see with the eyes of faith.

The catch is that they all thought they had sight. Remember the last line: "You see, you say, and your blindness remains." It comes to this. If we are unaware that we are blind, our blindness remains. It's like being so numb that we no longer realize that we are numb. That happens a lot. For example, we get so numbed by television and other communications media that we no longer realize our inner deadness. Until, perhaps, we hit rock bottom.

When we look at John's story, we notice the first blind people are the disciples. The sightless (faithless) disciples ask Jesus, "Whose sin was it? His sin or his parents'?" Jesus replies, "Look, you blind fools, it's neither his sin nor his parents' sin that made him blind." They are blind for thinking that God pinpoints people and makes them blind because of sin. Their idea is that God does it to punish them. Whose sin, is it that earns this punishment? It's either their sin or God's. The real blindness lies in their image of a punitive God, a God out to get them.

We still do that. Some believers do it with things like AIDS. They say, "See, God's getting them." God made them sick. God is punishing them. Jesus replies, "God doesn't operate that way. Neither he nor his parents sinned. He's just blind." If we could open our eyes, even in the blindness, the glory of God could be revealed.

The second blind group are the neighbors. "We think he was the one born blind. We're not sure. How could this be, that someone is blind from birth and now can see?" These neighbors are blind, because they're not open for surprise. Anything is possible with God. The gift surprises us when we expect it least. They are blind, because they had it all figured out. They had life in a box. "Things like this just don't happen in real life. Hollywood, yes, but in real life, blind people don't see." They are blind in their conviction about the way the world is. We can suffer from that kind of blindness, too.

The third blind group is the Pharisees, who knew and loved the letter of the law. They knew it well. They said, "Jesus, you can't do this, because of the Sabbath restrictions on any kind of activity." They were, you might say, "legally" blind. They were blinded by Jewish law. You don't heal on the Sabbath so you can't possibly be from God if you break the law. The letter of the law kills and legalism blinds. The Spirit sets us free.

The fourth blind group, the parents, said, "We're not sure it is our son." They're blind with fear. They defend themselves by saying, "Go ask him yourself, he is of age." They knew they could get expelled from the synagogue. We can be blinded by fear, too: fear of being different, fear of the truth, fear of life, fear of risking love, fear of gossip, fear of losing our money. And Jesus says, "You are blind." The only one who can see is the man born blind, because he allowed Jesus to give him sight.

We all live in some blindness. One way or another, we all have our blind spots. They're blind spots, because we don't know we have them. And if we say, "I have no blind spots," that's the biggest blind spot. Arrogance is a usual indicator of blindness. So in one sense, we are invited to see how, if we pay attention to Christ, the gift of God, we can allow God to waken us from our subhuman blindness. God can awaken us to a transparent holiness for which I think we are wired. But we can't free ourselves from our own blindness. The beautiful song, "Amazing Grace," says it well. It is by the power of grace that I know I was blind and now I see. Amen.

## Sin

Sin takes on clear and vivid meaning in this context of covenant and grace. If there were no sin, liturgy and its transformation would be entirely different. The liturgy takes sin quite seriously, putting a request for mercy up front. Our original sin is the refusal to be ravished by the gift of God. We want to be in control, so we hold within ourselves the reluctance to be loved, for fear of losing our self-control. The gift of God is universally given, but it is not so universally received. Many refuse to receive the gift. I watch the chronicle of refusal on the evening news. I know that even more intimately from within—I have refused the gift.

I remember a symbolic example. As a kid, I was stubborn. Once my parents wanted me to go to a birthday party at Mildred's house. I didn't want to go, but I went and I hated it. When we hate something, we reject everybody and everything by holding our breath. We get so caught up in ourselves that we're not going to receive anything. We take only what we want and then hold it all in. That was my mood, that was my scheme.

But, and I'll never forget this, Mildred was drinking some chocolate milk and started choking on it. Milk was coming out her nose! It was startling! The unexpected surprise took my held breath away! My resistance was melted and I enjoyed the party. (Maybe the elder brother of the prodigal son needed an experience like that when he refused to go to his father's party.)

My point is that sometimes even when we are in the rigidity of sin so we don't want to receive gifts and we are turned in on ourselves, life can deal out moments of surprise and grace that can shock us into a deep receptivity.

The liturgy is designed for us sinners. It is designed to present us with a vision of God so shocking, so generous in contrast to our armored breath-holding posture that we let go of our resistance.

Psychologists call these moments of *cognitive dissonance*. It means that we think one thing, and we see information that doesn't fit with what we already know. This discrepancy so jars us that we have to rethink in order to fit in this new information. It's like Isaac Asimov's definition of a good science fiction story. "There is one thing that cannot happen, must not happen, and is now happening." When that occurs, we are in a position to learn, to change, and to endure, albeit against our habitual outlook, that wonderful gift of transformation.

Sometimes those moments are painful, sometimes wonderful. Falling in love is such a moment. It's our big chance to be opened up. We see the world bathed in a light so pure it must be imported from paradise. I remember when my brother, Jack, fell in love. He stopped fighting with me. Fighting was now inappropriate to express himself. It was a gift to both of us!

But sometimes it can be terrible. A friend of mine recently died in a car crash at age 31. It was awful for the whole family and all his friends. His brother took it especially hard. His brother was one of those not fully open to the gift. But at the moment of his brother's death, he opened like a flower. A year and a half later, he still is open. On the phone the other night, he said he understood that in some way his brother died for him. His brother died, and now he sees the gift of life as he has never seen it before.

Life wakes us up, or tries to. The gospels keep telling us to be vigilant and stay awake, and the liturgy keeps shocking us with a vision of God's love for us that is calculated to keep us awake nights. We need to be awake to see that life is a gift. We keep coming to church to wake up. My poor aunt was always falling asleep. Bad liturgy does that. Good liturgy wakes us up. It allows us to keep vigil for the future in which the fullness of the gift will be given.

## Blindness I Have Known

Let's look at the life of Jesus, who invites us from blindness to sight, and see what he offers us as conversions—the move from blindness to sight. If we really eat and drink the bread and the wine, and take them into our hearts, then we let the Eucharist be a transformative process. If we eat this bread and drink this wine, we will be transformed from our blindness into full sight.

Many of us are subject to one or more of these blind spots. I'll begin with a story about my own blindness. When I was first ordained, I thought I had all the answers. I had been to school at the best Catholic university in the world, I did my theology at Louvain in Belgium, the oldest Catholic university, dating back to the 1400s. I had a great theological education, I was up on my Vatican II theology. I was ready! I went to a suburban parish in Saratoga, New York. I had the documents of Vatican II clutched in one hand and my hymnal in the other. And they were going to shape up! *Prophet* was not too strong a word. They were going to sing—my way—they were going to imbibe the finest in contemporary theology, and they were going to like it. I was super-priest, God's gift to the church.

Things got ugly, however. About one year into my act, a woman approached. (Later, I found out some of my friends had the same kind of encounter. Apparently, God uses this technique frequently.) She spoke with charming frankness, "When the hell (I'm quoting . . . ) are you going to get off your high horse? When are you going to be a human being like the rest of us?" You can imagine how I felt. She pointed out my blindness, but I didn't want to see it. After all, I was privileged. I was the eldest son of a good Italian–American family. I was white, educated, ordained, and celibate. In brief, it didn't get any better than that. I was like Lucy in "Peanuts." I was blind. I didn't see it at all. But this woman performed a valuable prophetic role for me. She invited me (with what I considered a certain abrasiveness) to dismount. It was a long climb down, and I was awkward, but conversion can be as fast as St. Paul's or as slow as mine. Learning how to be a human being took some time, and I still haven't completed the task.

You read the papers. You know that priests can be really clay-footed. All of us are broken, we're all part of the human race. Ordination does not guarantee holiness. Nobody is spared or denied transformation opportunities.

Then there was a previous conversion I experienced. I was only 20. I was church organist at St. Joseph's parish in downtown Schenectady. At 20 I played this great four-manual organ. I was a musician! I played the organ, I led the music, I was 20, I was making $2 a mass, and I thought I was pretty good.

Then, this 13-year-old kid was hanging around the organ one day. His name was Carl. I was 7 years older than Carl, and I thought I was hot stuff. Carl said to me, "You play real nice." I said, "Thank you." He said, "Can I try it?" I allowed him. "Sure, you can," thinking he'd be able to play a few notes.

He got on the organ, and I don't know what you know about organ technique, but he arranged the stops and began to play. That organ sang. It moaned, it screamed, it danced, and exulted from every pipe. He turned loose the toccata finale of Widor's Fifth Organ Symphony with notes flooding from every pipe. I was aghast. I couldn't even think about trying that toccata. And there was this 13-year-old virtuoso playing his heart (and mine) out! But you know what was going on inside me! I was, of course, thinking, "My that's a wonderful piece. . . ."But I wasn't really thinking, I was dying. A cancerous-green jealousy engulfed me. Rage. I wanted to shut down the organ and tell this upstart, "Get outta here, kid, go play some-place else. You bother me."

But something strange happened. I decided to take a higher road. I decided to be nice to him even though I was terribly threatened. This kid was going to take my job! I would be on the street, selling newspapers. Literally! I was threatened, jealous, and feeling terrible inside. Because when we become blind, our innards tell you something is wrong if we listen.

I remember what I did. I used to go to church every day and pray. So I was praying in front of the Blessed Sacrament, telling God how much I hated this kid, which is a kind of praying. The general theme of my lamentation was "God, why did you do this to me? Why did you send him? I don't like him." Then something inside my heart started to move. I realized I had to talk this out. So I went to confession, and it wasn't one of those scrupulous picky confessions I used to make, it was a serious heart-to-heart. I begin to see that I had an opportunity here. I could go either way. I had to choose between the conditional and unconditional. At 20 I had to make this terrible choice. I decided I had to let this pride out in confession. Well, this sacramental encounter worked. Carl and I became very good friends. I witnessed his wedding, he played the organ at my ordination and first Mass, and I baptized his children. We're still good friends, but I had to overcome my jealous blindness.

## Types of Blindness

Besides my own blindness, there are others I've seen. I'll arbitrarily categorize some types and look at the transformations Jesus can accomplish for us if we're open to the gift. If we allow the discipline of the liturgy to open us, we face these transformations and embrace their gift.

We sometimes feel that life is just one darn thing after another. That can get pretty blinding. Life is a problem to be solved. That's called a religious blindness. I call it *religious* because we think we are God enough to solve the mystery of life. We're going to figure out this mess, and when we get it figured out, we're going to have it all together. I think that's a real blindness. Ultimately it puts all the pressure on ourselves and our egos. When we look at Jesus, he says to be freed of that blindness, come into the light, the light of knowing that life is a gratuitous gift to be received—not to be figured out. All is grace. When that transformation occurs in us, then we can say we have become religious.

All world religions, not just ours, face this kind of blindness. The universal tendency is to think that we're in charge of this thing called life. All world religions lead the believer to surrender to life as gift. So in this blindness, a religious transformation is needed. I think it is the core of any kind of spirituality. My Buddhist friends agree. So do my Jewish, Hindu, and Muslim friends. (I ask my non-Christian friends to help me not to get too narrow in my understanding of the Mystery.) At the core of all their traditions is the insight and belief that life is gratuitous. We are blind if we think it can be figured out or controlled.

The second blindness is intellectual. This blindness prompts us to think knowledge is having all the facts. When we have the data, we have it all. We become blinded, overwhelmed by data. We get run over on the information super highway. I would suggest that having data is only the beginning of knowledge. Blindness equates the two. In one sense we got into that as a church with our educational systems. We're making some progress, to the extent that we know how we should do it, even if we can't, yet. Simple memorization of religious data does not give us faith.

We must distinguish between faith and beliefs. We can have a lot of beliefs and little faith. Faith is more an attitude of trusting surrender to God, beliefs are the data. The Pharisees had all the religious data, but seemed to lack faith. They knew the law, and they were blind. The conversion transformation that comes to us in Jesus is the realization and cherishing of the meaning of the data, not the data only. Conversion happens when we go deep into the meaning and mystery of things. We have been given an intellect to probe meaning and to be illumined. Data do not speak to the heart, meaning does. The transformation from the blindness of the intellect is to see that knowledge is meaning, not data. We must ask why. Jesus did and was crucified for it. Real religion is not knowing the facts, it's living in the meaning of that religious communion.

In short, Jesus came to take away our sins, not our brains. That's why we keep finding new ways of doing theology as we probe the data of our faith. We keep reformulating the meaning of the mystery. Our minds were made free by Christ, too, so we keep using them to situate our changing lives in the heart of our gift of God. So we continue to ask why, and the answer is always about meaning.

In the documents of the Second Vatican Council, the church asks why of itself and asks why of its tradition. Why do we do what we do? We had been getting a little closed. John XXIII talked about closed windows. Our tradition might be called our data. We had to ensure it didn't harden into merely historical data, so we asked why. As a church, we are in the process of conversion. When we opened up the windows, a marvelous metaphor for opening to the Spirit, we opened a new way of being church. We have to ask why. It is not a luxury option. We are wired with curiosity by God. We are wired for meaning, not just data.

If we don't ask the meaningful questions, we become or remain blind. The blindness can be collective, as in the case of religious or political institution, but sometimes it can be private and personal. Why do I stay in this marriage? Why do I let myself be abused—by husband or wife or parent or child or boss? Blindness sets in when we refuse to question. We are often afraid to question, because we believe things will change and questioning is always threatening. We are afraid to see. We may pay a therapist

$150 an hour just to help us ask the question. They sit and ask, "Why?" We are looking for some clarity. We're all looking for light. In light, we can see our way to move from data to meaning.

When you start probing, things transform. Maybe there's a question in your life that you are afraid to ask. That's all right. Don't ask it until you're ready. It's a powerful spiritual act, and you should not attempt it until you feel at least some confidence that you can pull it off. I know when I have questions I must ask, I face the prospect of everything inside me changing. I'm afraid. Don't do it prematurely. The time will be ripe when someone comes into your life and prays with you. Then floodgates will open and you will see.

## Blindness of the Heart

Then there is a blindness of feeling. We get stuck when we sit on our feelings and we don't acknowledge or claim them. We are humans, we have feelings. We can be blind and ignore our gut reactions to things. We swallow our emotions. Or we hide them. Men are sometimes taught not to show tears and women are sometimes discouraged from displaying anger. We have good reasons, cultural ones, for not revealing our feelings, but it eventually makes us blind. Our God encourages us to appreciate the gift with all our feelings so they have to be available. God does not want only an intellectual response to the gift of God's self. An affective, richly emotional response is demanded. Nothing else has the transformative power needed. Gratitude is from the heart. It can include tears, joy, pain, fear, anguish, and love. I suggest that many of us are stuck in our feelings, a kind of blindness of the heart.

When our feelings get stuck, they sour. Our God-given gift of feeling becomes a liability. For example, anger is a natural feeling. When it happens naturally, it lasts 10 seconds, maybe 20. But if it lasts all day, all month, or years, it is no longer productive. It means we're sitting on it, and it is festering. In childhood, many of us swallowed a lot of anger. We experience anger when a parent dies, a child dies, or because we were passed over for a job, but we sit on it, because "nice" people don't show anger. Anger is a God-given response when something has to change. That's why the adrenaline flows for those few seconds—so we muster the courage to say that something must change. However, if we sit on it, we become bitter. We become depressed, filled with hatred and a desire for revenge. We often become passive–aggressive, taking out our anger on inappropriate targets in ways that we don't acknowledge, because we're inwardly blind to our rage. We smile and stab.

Christ was angry in the temple. He said, "Something has to change here. You can't use my house of prayer as a den of thieves" (Luke 19:46).

How do we move from blocked feelings to a creative use of them so we build up the body of Christ in our family and our world? I was told one way once during spiritual direction. My spiritual director noted that I was sitting on a lot of anger. He said, "Here's a rubber hose. Go to your room. Take out the phone book. And there in the quiet of your room, let go. Scream it out, beat it out." I did that for two years. When anger is clogged inside me, I can't be a Christian. I quickly become passive–aggressive. So I work with the phone book, and when I do spiritual direction, I pass on the hose and the appropriate advice. It can be a tennis racquet, a pillow, it can even be sitting in church praying intensely, screaming at least inwardly, "God, why did you do this to me?"

Jesus never went blind. He allowed his feelings to flow like water from a fountain. So can we. In every parish, in every family, there are bound to be some old feelings festering away that have caused affective blindness. Maybe we need to consider looking for a spiritual director to help us deal with some of this. Are there family or friends toward whom you carry anger? It's a heavy burden. Maybe you could put some of that burden down before it ruins your sight.

If you can't find a spiritual director, at least talk it over with a friend. We are blessed if we have someone with whom we can talk over these deep hurts. It must be someone who won't judge us for the deep feelings of hatred we are apt to carry. They must understand and accept you as you are, even as they gently suggest some ways to change. You can't do this alone. We have been given to each other in grace for just such inner healing.

Not only anger can blind us. Jealousy is a natural emotion; it's there to move us to try our best so we can do what we see the other person is doing. If we sit on jealousy, it degrades into envy, and we begin to think thoughts of sabotage and look for chances to discredit and gossip. Such are the acts of blind people.

## Moral Blindness

We have moral blindness. This is thin ice. We are morally blind when we think our criteria are the "letter of the law." My criteria become my own self-satisfaction. Then we're blind. I choose to do what I do because the letter of the law tells me, or because I'm chosing to do what I'm doing to satisfy my own ego. Moral blindness happens all the time. We get stuck in ourselves. Even though it looks like I'm following an external law, it is really my set of laws. Things become black and white. I do something because I want to or because I'm told to—both are forms of moral blindness.

Christ sets us free so we can be truly free to decide. We no longer choose on the basis of ego satisfaction or a personal, arbitrary set of laws, but on the value of being the gift given away. When we are persons of gratitude, we can make decisions based on the values inherently in the law, rather than merely the letter of the law.

Sometimes, priests get tired of people going to confession with the letter of the law in mind. We hear so many adults confessing like children. We hear things like: "Bless me, Father, for I have sinned. I missed Mass on Sunday three times." "Well, why did you miss Mass?" "Well, because I was sick." "Don't you know that missing Mass on Sunday because you are sick is not a sin?" "Yes, Father." "Why are you confessing this, then?" "Uhhh, just in case." When we get scrupulous about the letter, that's pure egotism. We think if we obey the letter of the law, we save our own hides. Our church has a lot of work to do to develop a moral conscience that's transformed in the values of the spirit of the law. That would prompt us to confess the deeper sins, especially those that have an impact on the social systems of work, family, neighborhood, and government. Confessions and reconciliation are wonderful when their focus is more than a laundry list of childhood naughtiness. When confession is rooted in a vision of what life can be, when it includes the larger community, and when it ad-

*Transformed by the Gift*

dresses the offenses against values and gifts, it is an exhilarating experience. When it is literal and legalistic, it is childish and sometimes even neurotic. Confession needs a heavy dose of catechesis before it really removes our blindness. Confession is not a dump, it is an illumination.

Confession rooted in fear is especially poignant. When confession is made just so we won't burn in hell, it is always imperfect. It tends to be trivial and repetitive, as a blind ego tries to bribe an angry God that it fears. "Just in case" confessions sound a lot like the person is dealing with a traffic court judge, not a loving Father. To move from that to a conscience that sees the values of the law takes a lot of transformation and pastoral care.

One blindness is the scrupulous confession, the other is the person who doesn't go for years. They don't know what to say either, and sometimes they think they have never sinned. That's just as dim sighted. We need to deal with both forms of blindness.

## Images

Our image of God controls our lives to a large degree. Our religious imagination controls our hearts and emotional responses. If our image of God does not conform to what Christ wants it to be, a loving God, we can get confused and angry and lose hope. Then we block our feelings, wallow in despair, get angry forever, live by the letter of some kind of law, live in fear, and in general self-destruct.

Our next blindness involves our image of Christ. Who is Christ, anyway? We may think Jesus was a good guy who lived 2,000 years ago, and we should follow his example. That's not really who Jesus is. Our Christ is the Risen Lord who lives now. Where two or three are gathered in his name, he is present. He is the ocean in whom we live. Tertullian poetically describes us as the little fishes following the big fish. We breathe Christ, he is not a dead historical character. He is the presence among us now. Without living in that presence, we die like fish out of water. How can we be converted and transformed to know that presence so deeply that we are never alone? This Christ fills the universe and all its parts. There is no place we can go where Christ is not. We must change our hearts to see that presence. That's the mystical Christ. When we think he is just a good example, we reduce him to a mere historical figure. Like the man I heard of who said: "If Jesus knew what you were talking about, he'd turn over in his grave!"

### The Church

The church needs conversion, too. We've been trying to do this for 2,000 years, because the

*Transformed by the Gift*

church realizes its blindness. We used to think the church was a "they." Remember the sacred pyramid? God, pope, cardinals, archbishops, bishops, monsignors, pastors, assistant pastors, deacons, brothers, sisters, and finally the laity, first the men and then, holding up the whole triangle, were the women!

Sociologist Seymour Fischer looked at this triangle and observed "The more that women were suppressed on that triangle, the higher you got on the triangle, the more you dressed like a woman!" This quote is from his book *Body Consciousness*. He also notes that what we repress comes out in strange ways! In the church, we are in a time of transformation. The church is no longer "they," we are now realizing that the church is a "we," created and united by Baptism. We are ordered in a way that leads to communion. We share a common life of Baptism, a common priesthood, and through Holy Orders became an ordered communion in love.

The community is ordered but always for the sake of the community as the body of Christ. That's a big conversion. You see it in liturgy, you see it in parish councils, you see it in the way we share sacraments, you see it in the RCIA, in the multiplication of ministries— these are signs of recovery from a period of different perspectives.

As we recover from our blindness, we let go of the rigidities, we no longer exchange hatred with our Protestant friends, and we make friends with other religions. John XXIII opened some windows and hearts, but we're still struggling to find unity without insisting on uniformity. In the past, we insisted that Africans act like Italians, we forced Japanese and Chinese to say Mass like the Italians. That's not bad if you're Italian, but John XXIII said we have to let other languages praise God, and the people need to receive the gift in their own language, the language in which they make love, teach their children, shop, and express their feelings. Let them use the language in which they receive the gift of life to receive the gift of God in liturgy.

Now we see wonderful rituals coming from indigenous cultures worldwide. We seek unity without uniformity. To the extent we have that, we move from the pyramid to the circle of the people of God. That's a big conversion, but it's in process.

Are we baptized simply because we're afraid we're going to go to hell? I suppose that's OK, but even in the old catechism books, when we confessed our sins for that reason, it was called "imperfect contrition." "Because I dread the loss of heaven and the pains of hell." It wasn't perfect contrition, but it would at least get you time in purgatory. They did keep the significance of the real reason to be contrite distinct from what many settled for. We confess our need for God because of God's great goodness and love.

There is a conversion in baptism that Jesus shows us. We are baptized, because "you are all good and deserving of all my love." We are baptized, because we believe somehow that God has made us the beloved one. We have eaten the grain from the bins so that we can remain holy as God is holy. We are baptized to be God's chosen ones, holy and beloved. We are to be clothed with Christ, a holy priesthood, a royal nation, a people set apart so that through us the good news can come to all the Earth. Doesn't that sound much more visionary than the blindness we can get stuck in when we say we're only baptized because we're afraid to lose our souls?

We have been baptized, because God has called us. St. Peter says, God has chosen you from the beginning. By the blood of Christ you have been redeemed and sanctified and made holy so you can be a nation that proclaims the wonderful works of God and that, through you, God's creative energies might flow to all those who live in darkness and the shadow of death. That's a conversion. It's called a gospel conversion. Where are you blind? Where will you face conversion?

# 4.
# Awake to the Gift That Is in Us

*Now there are varieties of gifts, but the same Spirit; and there are varieties of services, but the same Lord; and there are varieties of activities, but it is the same God who activates all of them in everyone. To each is given the manifestation of the Spirit for the common good.*

*—1 Cor. 12:4–7*

$\mathcal{L}$et's begin with a paraphrased portion of a short story by Keith Davis, called "The Pause."

Worry and work had prevented a stressed and pressured executive from doing any serious Christmas preparation, even shopping. But in his line of duty, he had helped a woman in the company with personal problems, and she and her family expressed their gratitude several times.

On the afternoon of the Christmas party, she came into his office with a Merry Christmas wish and a series of gifts. He opened two or three gag gifts and then one box that was empty. She explained that she knew he was too busy, and she was offering him a pause. Just some blank time and space. She said he needed a pause.

He reflected years later that he had never forgotten the gift, and it was the gift he cherished most that Christmas. It was the one he used most often. He knew his life was too full, and he needed some leisure time, but he never bothered to take it until he received this beautiful symbolic gift. We all live by symbols, and they can reach us on levels that admonitions or good resolutions never do reach.

## Go in Peace

When we make a retreat, or drop into a quiet church, or claim an afternoon for reflection "just because," we take a pause. Maybe an hour, a day, perhaps even several days or more. A pause in our life can be any moment in which we learn to receive and believe, rather than just run and gun. We come to the feast of Christ refreshed after a pause. If we can become silent within ourselves while we pause, we become sensitive to and appreciative of the gift that God gives us in life and liturgy. We pause from our busy lives and praise the Lord and receive the bread and wine, the pause that comes when we are called to be transformed and we are stopped in our steps. We say, "This must stop. We must be changed." When we are

*Awake to the Gift That Is in Us*

## This Is My Body

To help see what Pius XII called the Mystical Body of Christ, I want you do a visual experiment with me. In my hand I have a loaf of bread, can you see it? Look carefully at this loaf. What do you perceive? Nourishment. When you see nourishment, what do you see concretely? Seeds. When you see seeds, what else do you see? Yeast. Those microorganisms are right here. What else? Flour. We need to have a farmer. So there's farmer in here, and a miller in here. And a mill and water. See it? We know all this, but sometimes we're so sleepy and unaware we don't see, our inward eyes are shut. We see salt, sugar, butter, and when we see butter, we see cows, . . . grass, heat—and, of course, fire. And when we see fire, we see ovens. To have seeds, we need soil. Now we can see the soil. And in the soil we have . . . worms. See the worms? If we are awake, we can see the worms. Besides worms what else in the soil. Fertilizer. What kind? Organic and inorganic! If you're awake, you see everything that is there. Sooner or later the whole digestive system is in this bread. Because the cycle will happen again. This bread doesn't come from nowhere. It comes from everywhere.

In one sense it is everything. If the mandatory label listed the real ingredients, we would know it contains air, sweat of the brow, our grandmothers, with all their memories. Where is this bread to go? It should go to all hungry mouths. To the poor, the children, the struggling in Bosnia, unlikely destinations unless we know all the ingredients.

We can even see the sun. When we see the sun, we see the stars and the black holes, and the whole cosmos. The scientists tell us that matter is neither destroyed nor created so there are atoms and molecules in here from our ancestors. Can you see? Now, hold this all together and stay awake. Hold everything you see in the bread in your hearts, because over all that the church says, "*This is my body.*"

Over all that bread, the church says, "This is my body. Take and eat." Take and drink. Stay awake. Over all that, the church says, "This is the body of Christ. It is the bread of life." Feel that. Because that's the Mystical Body of Christ. When we eat this bread, and we do not recognize the body, we eat and drink judgment to ourselves. I suggest that in order to go in peace, we must first realize and stay awake to the depth of bread, the ordinary that becomes extraordinarily ordinary for those who are awake enough to see the body of Christ.

Being in that body is the heart of the Christian. Being awake is being in the interrelationship of all things. With the appreciation of that gift of *interbeing* we become conscious of the many parts to this body with one spirit uniting us all. The eye can't say to the hand, I don't need you; therefore, you're not part of the body.

*Awake to the Gift That Is in Us*

identified some: some teach, some preach, some speak in tongues. Those were the kind of tasks and charisms in the spirit that he identified in his church at Corinth. What about your church? We cause ourselves unnecessary problems by thinking that to be good Catholics, we must do something concrete like working in a soup kitchen, or being a missionary. But we may not have a charism for that and may make a mess of it.

I suggest that somehow in our communities, if we want the Mass to end "Go in peace," we must have a mechanism for discerning the gifts. Perhaps some among us have that gift of discernment. I hope our leaders do! When we have access to that gift, we can say to one another, "You have this wonderful gift of being a teacher, why are you an usher?" or "You have this wonderful gift of being a reader, and you really don't have the gift to be in the choir. You have this wonderful gift of preaching, why don't you come and be a part of our retreat team for the teenagers. You really know how to organize media, you really know business, you've been given a mind to figure out how to subvert the system. Why don't you use it for God?" Do you understand the outlines of what I'm suggesting? If we think that the ministry of the church is just to go out and do something—we must be involved in this, that, or those—we may be spinning our wheels, or worse, going in the wrong direction, because that may not be where the Holy Spirit is asking us to go.

Maybe someone in your community simply has the charism to endure sickness with courage! That's a big charism. To witness the presence of Christ to the community can be our ministry. Our ministry displays courage when we do nothing other than being sick. Being sick without losing faith manifests the Christian mystery, even if this seems contrary to the rugged American ideal. When the people do this, they minister powerfully to us.

But there may be some who can and should engage in the soup-kitchen ministry, and can organize and provide direct services to the poor. Wonderful! Those gifts must emerge. Others have the gifts of being mothers and fathers. We must affirm those gifts and must not overtax those charisms by loading on such folks other tasks for which they have no charism.

We may have the gift of being an artist, and it may just flow out of us for the life of the community. It is almost as if these charisms within us all are the ways God's gift comes to the community. They really are not our charisms. We received them as gift, and in return, we share them with the community for the building up of the body until we recognize and know, in the mystical way I described. Over all this we say, "This is my body."

We say this until all creation is one, with all divisions healed, as we say in the Eucharistic prayer. Then we can sing God's praises through

Christ our Lord, from whom all good things come.

I suggest another task. Maybe we must, as a community, start engaging each other to work out a mechanism for the discernment of gifts. We must do this if we really are awake and if the feast is to effect a transformation in us as a Eucharistic people. When we do this as a community, not an organization, we support these gifts, and we don't rank one gift above another. That was Paul's problem in Corinth. This can be a hard thing to do. Sometimes I think I have a gift, but I might just have a liking for something. I might like to be a reader, because I like standing up in public. But a liking isn't necessarily a charism. This leads directly to the question of how to work with those wonderful volunteers who have offered to read but don't have the charism. Or maybe they have a hidden charism that needs to be cultivated. We need more than skill alone, we need the gift of discernment.

Once you know your charism, do it. Do it, and you will find it isn't *doing* it anymore; it's *being* it. When you can figure out the charism, let it be. Let it be you. Then it's not work, it's hardly a doing, you're simply being what you've been given for the life of the community and the world.

I'm blessed that my bishop discerned in me the charism of being a teacher. He said, "Richard, you have the charism of teaching." To teach, I needed further education. So I was sent off to school to be educated for the community. Then, when I was asked to teach in Chicago, the bishop said, "Go and use your charism." I've been fortunate in having a bishop with this gift of discernment.

Now, I must be very careful, because I'm talking to myself, too. There is something over-whelming about receiving gifts. We have to re-ceive them, not take them, we have to cherish and cultivate them. Once I take a gift for granted, I lose. Instead of being an educator, I become a public speaker. But I'm asking myself and you to search within and ask, "Where is my most valuable charism? How can I tell?"

Here's my answer. It's where you find your joy. Joy is itself a gift of the Holy Spirit. You'll know. When you're in it and when you're shar-ing it, it's effortless. It's like music. When you don't have the charism, you work at music—and it sounds like it. When you have it, you play music. Only when you play music does it sound right.

Just don't be narrow. There are many differ-ent kinds of charisms. It can be in cooking or car-ing, feeding, and nurturing someone. There's joy in that. If you're a great cook, then it isn't some-thing you have to do, it's not drudgery. My mother has this charism. "Eat something!" She doesn't *do* cooking, she *is* cooking!

Once we discern our charisms, we can use them together to build up our communities. Then, even the stones will rejoice. The poor

*Awake to the Gift That Is in Us*

will rejoice, as will the children and the abused. The unborn and all creation will rejoice, because, as a community, we are awake to the gifts that are given here. And we use them in harmony, because over all this we say, "This is my body." And in this symphony of charisms shared, God will be praised.

People like Mother Teresa never burn out, because in one sense she's not *doing* anything. She's *being* the empty vessel in which the gift of the Spirit is poured out for the life of the world. If you're getting burned out, it's frequently because you're not acting out of your charism. Get out of it. Do something else. How blessed are we if we can find our charisms and also earn our livings doing it. In the past, this was possible. My grandfather was a shoemaker. That was his charism. He had a gift for making shoes. He would make shoes for the little children who couldn't afford them and for the rich children whose parents could pay.

Now we have these crazy jobs that many of us hate—we eagerly await "hump day," and we "live for the weekend." Think of the saying "TGIF." Why do we talk this way? We aren't acting out of our charisms and the stress of going against the inner grain is killing us. We know that a statistically significant number of heart attacks occur at 9:00 on Monday mornings. We need to pay a great deal of attention to how we can use our charisms to earn our livings. Our charisms are not confined to church activity, even though we use this *church* word. Charisms should direct all our lives. God is interested in everything we do, so we are equipped for every moment and every type of community.

## The Hard Questions

Thirdly, for us to go in peace, we must be awake and dedicated to probing the mystery that is infinitely comprehensible. I suggest that we do that as a church by being willing to ask the hard questions as the prophets did. You'll notice that prophets are always marginalized in the church and community, because they ask the hard questions—those nobody wants to answer. Nobody even wanted to think we should ask them, because once you ask the question, the empire can collapse, and the body can be renewed, and the church can be transformed. The world can be transformed. Our families can be transformed. Our lives can be transformed. Sometimes being willing to ask those kinds of questions requires being committed to living the questioning life. I am happy when my students enjoy the questions more than the answers. Then I know I've done my job as a teacher. Because the more we understand the question, the deeper we go into the answer. Once we have an answer, we confuse it with having "the" answer. We think we don't have to ask the question anymore. I suggest that if we

*Awake to the Gift That Is in Us*

are awake, and if the gift is there to be given, it is a living Word. It keeps speaking newer and deeper insights at every turn of history and every turn of life.

One question is particularly effective. It's an "edge" question. When you assess your situation and evaluate what is happening, always push yourself by asking, "Who is being forgotten?" Who is being left out of the community life? Who can't quite run with the crowd? Every community and every group effort tends to have cracks. Who is falling through the cracks in your church? The prophets were always concerned about those who were marginalized in one form or other. Such prophetic questions lead to the possibilities of justice, mercy, and an equality of compassion.

Dedication to these questions invites us to probe more deeply into the mystery of Christ. They may be aroused in us by the Spirit. These questions of discernment of charism and of awakening to the mystical body—all of that is how we can go in peace. And someday, if we get it right, there will be peace on Earth.

## A Closing Story

This is my favorite St. Francis story. Once upon a time, St. Francis was walking through the Umbrian forest and he was asking himself the question, "O God, who are you and who am I?" He was always dedicated to edge questions. He got lost in the forest. After two days, he was hungry. So he prayed, "Oh God, please give me some food. I am hungry." No sooner had he prayed that prayer than he noticed a house at the edge of the forest. The house had a big sign with a lantern hung near it. The sign said, "Fresh bread baked here daily." So he ran up to the house and knocked on the door. He begged, "*Signora, per favore,* please, a little bit of this fresh bread baked here daily." She looked at him and said, "Excuse me, Father, but we have no fresh baked bread here. All we do in this house is make these signs."

The moral of the story? If we want to go in peace to love and serve the Lord, we have to do more in church than just paint signs so that we feel good and warm and nostalgic. We have to come to the feast. And at the feast, we will receive the gift, the overwhelming gift, we will be invited to transformation, and we will enter the dangerous place where the questions of the prophets will be raised. And we will be invited by the Holy Spirit to live our charisms. We will be called to bake the fresh bread daily. In our ordinary lives, even in the absence, in and out of the pause, until some day in that body, all divisions will be healed. On that day, people of every race and language and way of life will be gathered to share in one eternal feast with Christ our Lord, from whom all good things come. Amen.

*Awake to the Gift That Is in Us*